Copyright ©2018 Gina Myrie
All rights Reserved.

This publication may only be reproduced, stored or transmitted in any form or by any means, with the prior permission in writing of the publishers.

Condition of sale:
This book is sold subject to the condition that it shall not, by way of trade or otherwise, be lent, re-sold, hired out or otherwise circulated in any form of binding or cover other than that in which it is published and without a similar condition including this condition being imposed on the subsequent purchaser.
This book is sold on the understanding that the publisher is not engaged in rendering professional services and neither the publisher nor the author shall be liable for damages arising herefrom.

Published by
Patchwork Heart Publishing
Northampton, England.
patchworkheartpublishing@gmail.com
07872441851

ISBN 978-1-9999332-0-3

Illustration by © Grand Visual Designs Ltd

Features illustrations by:
Denzell Dankwah, Kaysha Russell-Francis
and peotry by
Zion Johnson, Hannah-Marie Mclean Pyle and
Tanya Maynard

Printed in the UK

This book is dedicated to my amazing husband, Ivor and my Fantastic Five, affectionately known as 'the Childge'.

Thank you for your support, encouragement and motivation. I love you guys to the max! You are my inspiration and my blessing and for that, to God I am extreemly grateful.

To Purposeful Living.
When we understand, acknowledge and actively pursue the reason for our personal existence, we become an unstoppable force of greatness. Unmoved by criticism and negativity, strengthened by destiny and direction.

Discovery:
the action or process of discovering or being discovered

Definition: Oxford dictionary

CONTENTS

WORKING YOUR WAY THROUGH	IX
ACKNOWLEDGEMENTS	XI
PREFACE	XIII
INVESTING IN THE FUTURE	XVI
I AM WOMAN	1
THE ORIGINAL ME	2
DISCOVERY	8
TO THE FUTURE	10
WHO AM I? *BY HANNAH-MARIE MCLEAN PYLE*	11
TESTIMONY	12
CHILDHOOD CRY	14
REFLECTIONS	16
WORTHY	18
BAD SEED	19
ILLUSTRATION *BY DENZELL DANKWAH*	20
BAD SEED ACTIVITY	21
ACTIVITY 1:	22

ACTIVITY 2:	23
A LACK OF UNDERSTANDING	27
TRANSITION	28
THE RED PILL	32
IT'S ALL ABOUT CHOICE	34
AWAKEN ME	36
BEYOND POSSIBILITY	38
PHASES	41
LOVE	50
WHAT IS LOVE?	52
NATURE OF LOVE *BY ZION JOHNSON*	54
LOVE REVOLUTION	55
LOVE SPEAK	56
SAY MY NAME	58
ILLUSTRATION *BY KAYSHA RUSSELL-FRANCIS*	59
BY CANDLE LIGHT	60
THE ONE	62
FRIEND	64
BABY GIRL	66
SOMETIMES; LOVE HURTS	68
ACTIVITY 3	69

IDENTITY	81
I AM	82
WALKING BLIND	84
PURPOSE FILLED BEAUTY	85
A WOMAN FOR EVERY SEASON	87
MORE THAN ENOUGH	89
BEAUTIFUL YOU *BY TANYA MAYNARD*	92
ILLUSTRATION *BY DENZELL DANKWAH*	95
OVERCOME	96
RAINBOW	97
PURPOSE PRINCIPLE	103
VALUES	104
ACTIVITY 4	105
SOLDIER	112
WALK IN POWER	114
COMPASSION'S GAME	116
CRISIS	118
MAKE A START	120
GOD	130
BLESSED IS THE ONE WHO FINDS WISDOM	132

DISCOVERING EARTH *BY HANNAH-MARIE MCLEAN PYLE*	133
THROUGH GODS EYES	134
AFRAID	136
DEEPER	139
ILLUSTRATION *BY DENZELL DANKWAH*	141
WRAPPED UP	142
CHRISTIAN REBUKE	144
TESTIMONY REVISED	147
ACTIVITY SHEETS	157
COMING SOON...	162
ABOUT THE AUTHOR	164

WORKING YOUR WAY THROUGH

Discovery, Love, Identity and God is a book about personal discovery and growth written mostly in the poetic form.

Divided into the headings above, each section begins with an introduction and ends with clear pages for you to write your thoughts or revelations and space to have a go at writing your own poems.

You will also find short activities to engage thought around the barriers and doorways to your success. *(For more information visit ginamyrie.com)*

It is not necessary to work succinctly through this book as each poem stands alone, however it may be advantageous to do so for fluidity of thoughts.

Writing is an amazing way to clear the mind and to gain clarity, so I hope you feel inspired enough to fill the blank pages, creating a personalised journal and the beginnings of a personal development tool.

Gina Myrie

LOVE:
an intense feeling of deep affection.

Definition: Oxford dictionary

ACKNOWLEDGEMENTS

As always, I first acknowledge my creator, who designed me in his image with an unstoppable ability to achieve greatness. Thank you Lord for inspiration, vision, for hope, fulfilment and your Agape Love.

Acknowledging my mom for the frequent reminders that writing is a gift and within that, lies success.

Burt, Db, Nad, SimSimma, Curtis, Juice and Laz. I know I don't say it much but thank you for just being there! Life has its ups and downs but I am the fantastic person I am now because of you!... *(yeah i said fantastic lol)*

Tanya Maynard, thanks for trusting me with your poem and for the syntax support lol

And finally, to the late Colin Hines, aka Uncle Colin; though the conversation was brief the impact was strong. Thanks for taking the time to impart possibility. For being my Poetic role model. The time for you to publish your book ran short but as promised, here is mine.

IDENTITY:
determining who or what a person or thing is.

Definition: Oxford dictionary

PREFACE

As a parent, we try our utmost to give our children all the love, attention and guidance that they need but as we fumble our way through this unknown journey, it is likely that we will make mistakes. Mistakes that we hope will be bypassed and placed into the vault of unimpressionable actions. For many this is the case but for others, like me, the consequences of human imperfections can be detrimental to an individual's sense of value and worth.

In spite of the facts, I grew up feeling unloved, isolated and worthless and though on the outside people would have perceived me as being happy or confident, really it was all an act. I was a mess! Always a little too big to feel beautiful or attractive, not quite clever or talented enough, and born the wrong gender to be free to do the things I really enjoyed, like building, climbing trees and playing on the Nintendo 64 or the Sega Master System.

I grew up in a semi Christian house hold and attended a church who regularly reminded its congregation of their responsibly to 'live right' or 'end up in Hell'. All this alongside the typical west-Indian 'belt beating' for punishment should you do anything wrong. I grew up afraid. Afraid to determine my own identity always trying to attain the things I felt were missing, setting extremely high unattainable expectations for myself in the hope that all the attention I felt I missed would be restored to me by achieving something exceptional.

The problem is that childhood feelings do not merely go away with age, they often become the blueprint on which we base the rest of our life unless they are addressed.

We have to go through a journey of honest discovery to find our true identity which enables us to no longer be controlled by the perceived opinions of others but to live our impending years in freedom, happiness and purpose.

This book, whether good or bad, whether liked or not is in part, a snippet of my journey to me and an encouragement for you to pursue freedom and destiny without fear.

GOD:
the creator and ruler of the universe and source of all moral authority; the supreme being.

Definition: Oxford dictionary

INVESTING IN THE FUTURE

If I were to select a theme tune to represent my thoughts surrounding life it would be, 'The greatest love of all' by the late Whitney Houston. The lyrics simply say...

> 'I believe the children are our future
> Teach them well and let them lead the way
> Show them all the beauty they possess inside
> Give them a sense of pride'

So often I look into a world that seems to be crumbling under the pressure of mere existence. Family structures are breaking down, divorce and separation are common place, parents are often too busy to parent leaving children to be educated by the lyrics of musical icons or the lure of an interactive gaming system. Social media and its constant barrage of violence, sexualisation and unrealistic perceptions of beauty, wealth and success are becoming 'the community' in place of physical interaction. Services for children and young people are often withdrawn and violence, disunity and death have almost become a social expectation. We are a society that have become so numb to crime, life without morals and the normalisation of negative behaviours that we do not realise how much better things can be.

I want to live in the better!

I believe the children are our future and what they are taught whether consciously or subconsciously become the foundations on which the next generation is built and the structure in which the rest of us either thrive, suffer or learn to merely endure.

The future truly is what we make it, so why not make it great?

I believe that if we input the knowledge of personal value and worth into each child, and of their necessary existence, they are able to become the best versions of themselves beginning a cycle of positive change within our communities.

Changing the future doesn't have to mean grand gestures, inspiring a generation doesn't have to cost that which we do not have. It can begin with a simple conversation or acknowledgement of talent or value. If we all do our part, as big or small as that may be we become instigators of change and positive growth.

Within this book are a selection of poems and illustrations by talented young people. I wanted to use this opportunity to encourage them to dream big, not to get stuck in the mundane or the norm but to use their gifts to live out their potential and leave a positive imprint on the communities they interact with.

Denzell Dankwah, Kaysha Russell-Francis, Zion Johnson and Hannah-Marie Mclean Pyle well done. Your work is exceptional!

Thank you for taking the time to enrich this book with your amazing talents.

Investment:

An act of devoting time, effort, or energy to a particular undertaking with the expectation of a worthwhile result.

Definition: Oxford dictionary

Discovery Love Identity and God

I AM WOMAN

Woman
Beautiful Woman
Beautiful, Elegant, Distinguished Woman

Woman
Youthful Woman
Youthful, Brilliant, Resilient Woman

Woman
Virtuous Woman
Virtuous, Elected, Protected Woman

Sensitive Woman,
Fruitful Woman,
Extra – Ordinary Woman

I am woman!

THE ORIGINAL ME

I'm a black Christian woman,
I'm not a size 10
I'm voluptuous and luscious
Got mad skills with a pen.

I've fought every battle
with a lyrical spill
combat each attack
with a spiritual quill.

I've got powers of discernment
I'm a woman of steel
I'm a Nubian Poet
that's my signature seal.

I'm a mother of distinction
of honour and class
dignified in aura
with a little hit of sass.

I laid a foundation
of distinction within
so I rise to the top
I strive, I win!

I'm a whirlwind
protecting my world, my sphere
I'm a conqueror
I let no adversary near.

I am tender
But don't mistake my calmness as weak
I'm a lioness
I roar
I'm a revolution when I speak!

DISCOVERY

Life is undoubtedly the most complex, complicated and unpredictable journey we will ever travel. No matter the distance or destination we are guaranteed to encounter varying terrains, the highs and lows, the rough and the smooth and though often tiresome, the longer our journey the more opportunities we have to refuel, assess, re-assess, refresh and restart.

We are beings created for community and companionship, we cannot even make it into this earth without the coming together of two yet each of us is an exclusive issue with a destiny designed for one.

Every journey is different because our road map is internal. It is hidden within the uniqueness of each individual mind. There is a navigation system delicately infused within the aroma of each soul and in order to live out our potential it is important that we ingest that truth. It is imperative that we take the time to break free from the hypothetical chains that bind us to community expectations, to overcome the battlefield of the mind and invest the time into personal discovery.

It is when we know who we are that we are able to walk in power. That we are able to impact and influence our sphere and beyond. It is in this discovery that we find freedom and happiness.

"The process of discovery can be scary but necessary to understanding your current position, securing a clear space to move forward from."

TO THE FUTURE

The beauty of discovery
The endlessness of time
The past has lost its bond
The future is now mine

Nothing has been wasted
Learning is gift
Activating power
The next predicted shift

Discovering the beauty
Commencing life a new
Dreams no longer sacred
For each is coming true

WHO AM I?
BY HANNAH-MARIE MCLEAN PYLE
Age 10

Who Am I?
Born in Britain but I've been to France
Grandad's from Guyana
Grandma's from St. Lucia she's also been to Dubai
But who am I?

Visited their countries
They were both super hot and filled with love.
I met so many cousins, guess how many I've got?
1, 2, 3, 4, 5, 6, 7, 8, 9, 10 and more, more, more!
But the question in my brain remains the same
So, who am I?

I've travelled the world, or so I've been told
But there's an answer to a question I still cannot mould
Who am I?

TESTIMONY

I was messed up, confused,
misused and abused,
and I refused to believe
I was worthy of simply being me.

I felt oppressed and ashamed
so, I blamed the world for my life
Me, a Mother, a Wife.
Still craving to be a child,
acting wild, for attention and misplaced affection.

I became suppressed and distressed,
confined, unassigned,
diseased but blind to the cure,
surely there is more to life than this?

I yearned inside, burned because of pride,
behind which, destruction resigned,
until my eyes were opened to the truth.

Creation created me,
not broken but perfectly
filled to capacity
with a destiny no other can achieve,
equipped with every skill I could want or need.

Impossibilities fade,
possibilities made into reality,
God's specialty,
defining the beauty of me,
refining the image I now see.

CHILDHOOD CRY

Why is it no one hears
when you really want them to?

Why is it people recognise
all the wrong you do?

Why is it I can never shout
my feelings out aloud?

Why is it that I have a dad
who seems forever proud?

Why is it that I feel I've lost
the only gift I had?

Why is it things get worse
whenever I feel sad?

Why is it that I'm bothering
to write this poem down?

Why is it when I want to smile
my face gives off a frown?

Why is it that I find it
so hard to relate?

Why is it that the ones I love
are wrong but yet so great?

Why is the person in the mirror
disappointed at what they see?

Why is this disappointment
embedded deep in ME?

(1998)

REFLECTIONS
[just like you]

I'm just like you!
The way I look
The way I feel
The way I act
it's just unreal
We're so alike
I am afraid
that due to spite
I will ignite
into a flame
of rage and anger
burning bright
and though I know
it's hard to fight
despite my will
and all my might
I can't ignore
the things I saw
which are the reasons I war
within myself,

to keep me calm
and safe from harm.
For in my dreams
there is just rage
on every line
of every page
and now I'm torn
so deep within
I try to cover
all my sin
with outward smiles,
speech and words
that never threaten to disturb
my peace of mind,
which is surreal
but it's the part I wish were real
for if it were then I would feel
the way I want when revealed
into the mirror I would see
the perfect person looking back at me.

WORTHY

My soul cries out but my body is dead
Help me, love me, show me,
that I'm at least worthy of that.

Cleanse me, support me, heal me
Convince me,
that I'm at least good enough for that.

Tell me that your proud of me,
that my weight isn't all you see,
Don't let that define me
For who I am is more.

So, explore what is within me,
Respect me enough to help me,
Reveal my ability
For surely, I am worthy of that.

Don't compare me
but encourage my individuality,
Unite with me,
So I will no longer be needy but free!

For surely I am worthy of that.

BAD SEED

Implanted, a seed of destruction
the words the construction of the lie.

Deception manifests its intention
to destroy as time goes by.

Prevention is now unattainable
as the present overtakes the past.

Life has become sustainable
but we're susceptible for it can't last.

Embedded the seed of destruction,
as the weeds entangle the truth.

The lies increase expanding,
causing perception misuse and abuse.

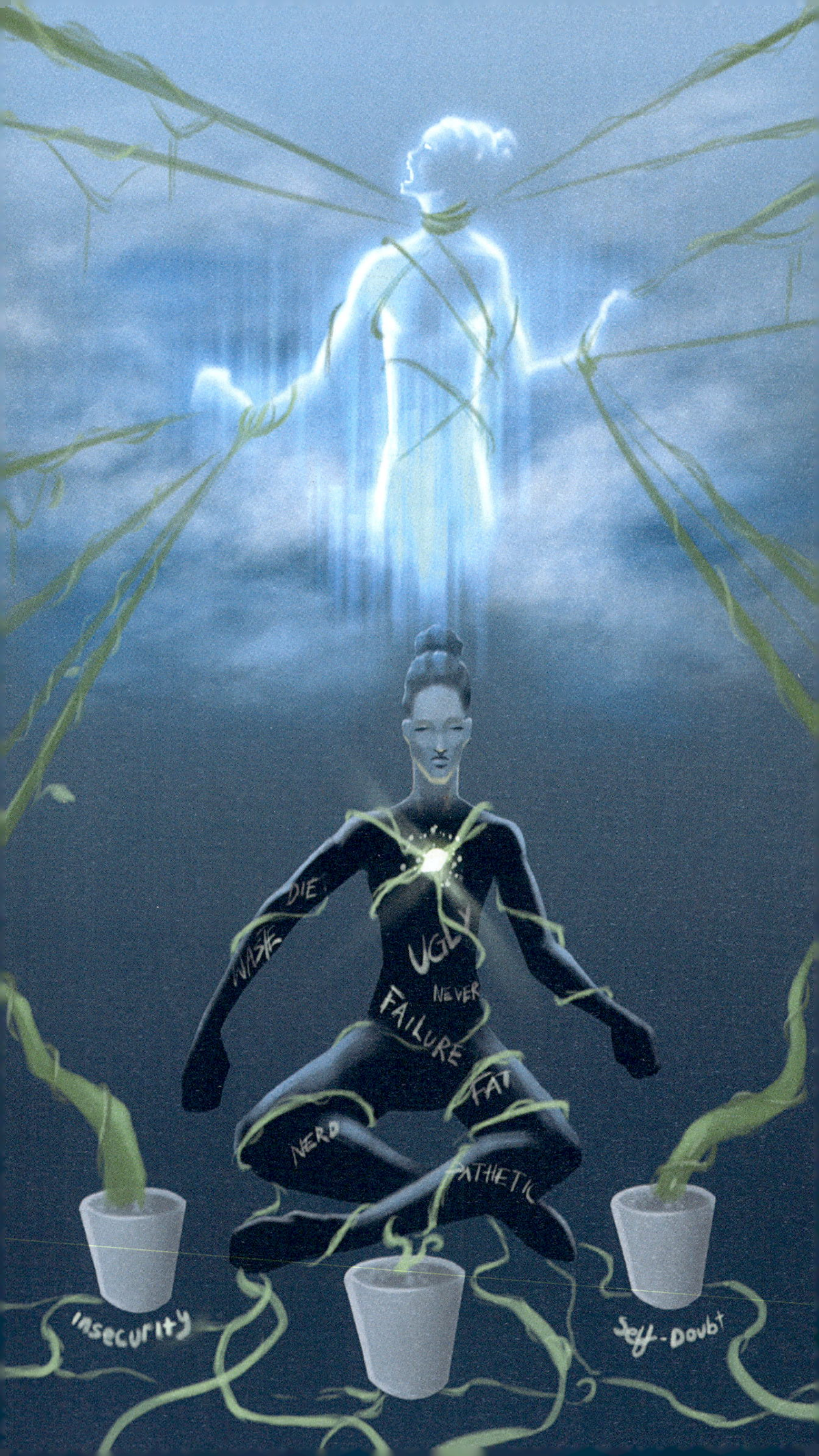
DIE
NEVER
FAILURE
FAT
NERD
Insecurity
Doubt

BAD SEED ACTIVITY

What are the 'bad seeds' that have been planted within your life, that are hindering your progress?

These seeds may have been planted at any time by any person but usually by the people you look up to or want to please the most; family members, partners, teachers, or friends.

One of the biggest seeds for me was being called 'fat' and the negative connotations that came along with that word.

I allowed the perception behind the word stop me from participating in certain sporting activities even though I loved sport. I would never go on a trampoline, attempt gymnastics or rock climb for example, because I was afraid of what people would (and did) say or think. I then focussed so hard on this word that it grew into a self-fulfilling prophesy. Losing weight has been one of life's greatest challenges ever since.

The way to root up these now 'fully grown' weeds is to identify them and accept that these words are merely opinions not facts. In fact, the only power they have is what you give them.

If you choose to continually water and feed negative thoughts by declaring them over your life (I'm fat, I'm an idiot, I'm ugly) of course they will grow and eventually overtake you presenting in the forms of depression, illness or poor mental health.

ACTIVITY 1:

Have a think about the bad seeds in your life. What are the negative things people have said or done to make you believe a lie about yourself?

List them below.

_____

_____

_____

_____

_____

_____

_____

_____

_____

_____

ACTIVITY 2:

Use your list to complete the table on the following page. This will form the beginnings of an action plan towards permanent positive change.

If you are struggling to create action points for yourself, use or adapt the suggestions below.

- I WILL FEEL THE FEAR AND DO IT ANYWAY

- I WILL SPEAK POSITIVE AFFIRMATIONS TO MYSELF EVERYDAY (EG. I AM BEAUTIFUL, I AM INTELLIGENT)

- I CHOOSE TO FORGIVE (THE MORE I SAY THE WORDS ALOUD THE MORE REAL THEY WILL BECOME).

- I WILL JOIN A SLIMMING GROUP

- I WILL WRITE A JOURNAL

- I WILL MAKE A LIST

(a free downloadable version of this table can be found at ginamyrie.com)

Bad Seed	Negative Consequence	Action
	What actions has this belief either stopped you from doing or caused you to do?	what actions can you take to break these negetive beliefs?
eg; You're too fat	*Embarrassed and afraid to take part in sporting activities, which in actual fact I love*	*Feel the fear and do it anyway. I joined a netball team*

Bad Seed	Negative Consequence	Action
	What actions has this belief either stopped you from doing or caused you to do?	what actions can you take to break these negetive beliefs?

A LACK OF UNDERSTANDING

A lack of understanding is my restriction!
As I evolve within this place
I move no further forward
I await a call, a sign
and though signs come and go
they pass me by.
Frustration is all I contain,
Anticipation becomes my weakness,
It seems the more I look ahead
is the more looking ahead is all I do.
I am surrounded by uncertainty,
Coerced into false security,
Forced to believe that I am free
when in reality insecurity contaminates me
I stand tormented by expectations,
Imperfections plague the serenity of my actions
I become a prisoner of self

TRANSITION

For me, one of the most challenging transitions is moving from 'given knowledge' to 'acquired truth'. It is challenging because it is scary. The idea that what we think we know, that the principles we have built our lives upon maybe saturated with misguided truth is extremely destabilising. However, it is something we need to address to live out our full potential.

From the moment we are born, we are fed knowledge, our liberty is stripped, and our programming begins. Our parents/ caregivers impart their ideas of right and wrong and we are subconsciously prepped on socially acceptable norms.

We enter the educational system where our programming is both reinforced and extended. We are taught how to streamline our learning to fit the brackets defined by a political system. To embrace the definition of intellect displayed by a score on a test designed to segregate, placing ourselves and others in hierarchical categories of 'ability' and 'potential'.

We are influenced by our church on the acceptable behaviours of 'Godly Living' which are often based on fear. We then use all our collated information to create an image of perfection the majority of us can never live up to. Corrupted by ideals we develop symptoms of a misguided truth, of a fake reality: Confusion, low self-worth, low self-esteem, unbelief, aimless, unfulfilling wonderings, ever hoping for the reality of a dream we have no actual faith we will make real.

We are told that creativity is merely a pastime. As long as we stay inline and are obedient to the systems we are rewarded with treats of money and status. Let me tell you that this is not living in freedom this is an excellently executed slave trade!

You see, a lack of understanding is our restriction. As we evolve and grow, we lose ourselves even more. We are often so focused on what we have been taught that we forget the importance and power of discovery and truth.

I believe that every individual is born with a purpose, born to leave a lasting and positive mark on this earth, but in order to experience the fullness of this existence, we need to go back to the beginning. To identify the origins of our DNA and relearn who we were born to be before entering the worlds programme.

As a christian, this even means in relation to what we know about Christ and what it means to serve him. We need to wipe out religiousness and traditionalism and begin to understand the bible in context. Not as a book used to reinforce life rules dictated by people but as a book that shows us the heart of God, a book that speaks life only whilst coupled with an honest relationship with Him.

One of my favourite films is the Matrix. Whilst sitting in a kind of holding room the main character Neo, has to make a potentially life/ reality changing decision. Does he take the blue pill and return to 'given knowledge' or take the red pill and begin to live in 'acquired truth'? I believe that knowing God and understanding that we were designed and created like him is where the basis of freedom lies.

Imagine if we understood that we give life to everything that we say, that every time we speak negativity into ourselves or others we make it real. Imagine if we knew that our passion and purpose had greater earning potential than our 'survival' career. Imagine if we knew that labels like dyslexia only exist because the brain is too wonderfully creative to fit within a controlled spectrum. Imagine if you knew that you're 'silly idea' was the beginning of an idea that was going to end starvation and malnutrition in the world. Imagine if we knew that all the miracles Jesus performed were minimal in comparison to what we can now do because of His example.

My request is that we acquire truth! If you seek out knowledge you will find it! The thing is that once you discover your truth, what will you do with it?

"I took the red Pill! Question is... will you take it too?"

THE RED PILL

I took the red pill
Oh my gosh, everything looks so bright
Literally the world is so light

I took the red pill
I'm reaching out and everything seems so real
I finally understand I have the power to heal

I took the red pill
I'm standing still and I'm embraced by the air
I literally can do all I dare

I took the red pill
I'm exploring, I simply can't resist
In this place, failure does not exist

I took the red pill
I've seen the gifts God has in store for me
And every one is labelled 'I am free'

I took the red pill
Prosperity and unimaginable wealth
Joy, happiness, peace and immaculate health

I took the red pill
Negativity has no legal resting place
Fear and hatred are an underpopulated race

I took the red pill
Honestly it feels as if I'm living in a dream
It's hard to believe, things are as perfect as they seem.

I took the red pill
I must admit, I do have one regret
Not having persuaded you to go and try it yet

IT'S ALL ABOUT CHOICE

It's all about choice
Whether you win or loose
If you wish to be defined
By another man's shoes
Or create your own way
And design a new box
With no restraining sides
Or invisible locks

It's all about choice
Whether you laugh or you moan
If you live with a heart
Made primarily of stone
Or enjoy every moment
As experience increased
Or mundanely exist
As the living deceased

It's all about choice
Whether you drive or you walk
If you travel at all
Or seize up at 'lets talk'
If you raise your desires
And crave what you say
Or carpe diem
And seize the day

It's all about choice
Whether you decide to believe
To remain in your mess
Or take measures to leave
To reap what you sow
Therefore lay down good seed
To harvest potential
For the earth is in need

It's in need of your intellect,
Creativity and vision
It's in need of your power,
Your strength is provision
It's in need of your talent
Your inimitable skill
It's in need of your greatest
To pursue its planned will

It's all about choice
Whether you win or loose
If you wish to be defined
By your own brand of shoes
If you wish to succeed
And become your life's boss
To at least try is gain
but to do nothing is instant loss

AWAKEN ME

Awaken me oh Lord.
Let me understand this condition.
The affliction of these systematic lies
is way too great.

They aggravate my mind.
Bombarding my soul,
these infectious deceits
effortlessly role
off the tongue of those deemed mighty.
Those considered powerful.
The so called intellectual.

Those influential bigots rage unapologetically,
spewing verbal diarrhoea
directly into the ear of the young,
the impressionable,
of the desperate, desolate and afraid.
In fact, even incantations are made upon the wise.
Upon nations primarily set apart.

Yet it is an art form of the wicked to deceive those who should know better.

They devise the letter of the law
into which they pour unproven facts,
theoretical spats of chronological nonsense,
unfortunately deemed as foundational knowledge
in which we abolish spiritual instinct,
or supernatural data
and instead cater to fiction and drivel.

We believe what we are told
never attempting to unfold the mystery,
delving into the history of the very beginning.
For example, we learn the earth is a ball
although we never seem to fall from the sky.
Have you ever wondered why that might be?
Or considered the possibility
that the world could be flat?
That conspiracy is truth
and schooling is simply a pat on the back for obedience
and playing the game.

Remaining in ignorance is an option
but adoption of consideration and deliberation
provide a much more truthful summation.

BEYOND POSSIBILITY

I want to experience beyond possibility
Envisage the things the eye can't see
Ponder on the edge of an atmospheric cloud
Travel faster than light and sound

I want to dive through the sea, to the ocean floor
To radiate peace in the midst of war
Be transported through space, break the barrier of time
Successfully conquer a mountainous climb

I want to sprint through a field in minimal clothes
Feel the breeze in my face and the earth through my toes
Open my mouth and sing like the stars
Collect colourful sand in tempered glass jars

I want to hibernate in winter in a forest tree home
And dine at a table crafted in stone
To dance in the rain as my life soundtrack plays
To lose myself in a spiral hedged maze

I want to step through the looking glass and see what's inside
Discover the world that exists in my mind
To engage my reflection and see how she performs
To shatter the rules of societal norms

I want to gather up suffering and throw it away
To glide through the air as night covers day
To slide down the rainbow and swim in pure gold
To capture the words of a story untold

I want to float on a physical example of love
Paint visions of hope on the wings of a dove
Blow bubbles of joy as my tears wash out pain
To know I've done good as I finish life's game.

I want to clutch at the things the eye can't see
And unravel the impossible's possibility.

"The Impossible is only impossible until it is achieved"

PHASES

Life has its phases
Some good and some bad.
So many stages
Some joyous, some sad.

Experiences taint us
Yet force us to grow.
Overly cautious
Yet eager to go.

Realisation gains reason,
Understanding kicks in.
Personality treason
Confliction within.

Emotive occasions
Hormonal debates
Internal frustrations
External constraints.

Deceptions uncovered
Relationships change
Independence discovered
Past truths rearranged.

LOVE

LOVE

Love. Though the word itself is simplistic in structure and formation, its content is vast, full of power and interwoven complexities.

Four letters: That when put together are regularly thrown around in verbal confession and affirmations, in poetry, prose, verse and rhyme. A word that in action is imperative to wholeness and fulfilment yet, the tangibility of its essence seems to avail many.

Love is the reason for both heartbreak and internal elation, it is the foundation for peace and a springboard for hope yet it is becoming an endangered necessity replaced by lust and desire.

Love, literally makes the world go round but it seems the conspiracy to rid the world of love may be true. If love is watered down then so too is compassion and community, making way for the growth of envy, fear and hatred for oneself and one another.

If love is watered down, then so too is hope and the possibility for change.

If love is watered down, then so too is the very humanity that we exist in, ultimately leaving us as individuals left longing for personal completion, ever wanting more, never satisfied or truly happy.

Love needs to succeed this worlds system of perceived power because it is THE POWER to transform what we think is good, into actual perfection.

WHAT IS LOVE?

Love is patient, love is kind. It does not envy, it does not boast, it is not proud. It does not dishonour others, it is not self-seeking, it is not easily angered, it keeps no record of wrongs. Love does not delight in evil but rejoices with the truth. It always protects, always trusts, always hopes, always perseveres
Love never fails.

1st Corinthians 13: 4-7

The Love Revolution is near.

"Imagine who I would be if one day I woke up knowing without doubt, God loves me."

NATURE OF LOVE
BY ZION JOHNSON
Age 10

When people think of love
They think marriages and doves
But if you look down deep
You may think that you're a sheep
You see, love here is the key
It helps us live in harmony
Bees here are an example
People think they're harmful
But, when you look in the nest
They really are the best
So be more like the bees,
I'm not saying live in trees
I mean, live and learn together
And we can spread the peace

LOVE REVOLUTION

Love is a vibration
It is the heat beat of Joy
It's the birthmark of creation
It's the power to destroy

It's the authority to heal
It's the cannon of peace
Its existence made real
It's freedom's release

It's the attitude of empathy
It's the executioner of shame
It's the opponent of apathy
It's the comforter of pain

It's the glass of vulnerability
It's the confinement of fear
It's mercy's facility
Its revolution is near!

LOVE SPEAK

When we speak of love, what do we really mean?
Is it the type of love we've seen
Portrayed upon a big screen
When he meets her and she meets him
And oh… they feel so tingly within
And the sky is so blue
And the grass is so green
And he makes you feel like you've just got to scream
But hold on, haven't I just seen
Your love over there kissing Pauline…
Where has your love been?

When we speak of love what do we really mean?
Is it the type of love found
At the bottom of a tub of ice-cream, maybe
Or in a nice Yorkshire tea
Or maybe in a chocolate from Mr Cadbury
And it makes you feel whole
And it makes you feel one
Till you stand on the scales and
1,2,3 pounds you've put on…
Where has love gone?

When we speak of love, what do we really mean?
Is it the type of love that whispers I do
To honour and obey, "yes I do take you"
But then two become three and three become four
And the life you once had

Has now run out the door…
Love is becoming a chore

What do we really mean when we speak of love,
Could it be all of the above?

Unsure?
Then let me show you where true love is found.

It's found in a tear descending to the ground
Which is caught in the palm of an invisible hand
It's the cushion of grace under bended knee
Supplied as a gift for both you and me
Its unconditional, with no beginning or end
It's a father, brother, saviour and friend.
It's the sacrifice of life for another unknown
It's the willingness of one, to defer his throne
It's the image of a cross, steeped in blood
Engraved with the message
Jesus is Love

SAY MY NAME

I don't begin to presume that every woman's the same,
But for me, I just need you to say my name.

With all passion and pride, I need you to be the one
Declaring my beauty compareth to none.

I need you to gaze in my eyes and be lost in their pull
To speak to my heart till my love tank is full

Lay down with me, cover me with your irrefutable strength
Desire me beyond an immeasurable length.

I need you to guide me, protect me, send shivers down my spine
Let the hairs on your skin respond only to mine

To crave my touch and to melt as we kiss
To embrace me and hold me even if I resist.

I don't begin to presume that every woman's the same,
But me, I just need you to say my name.

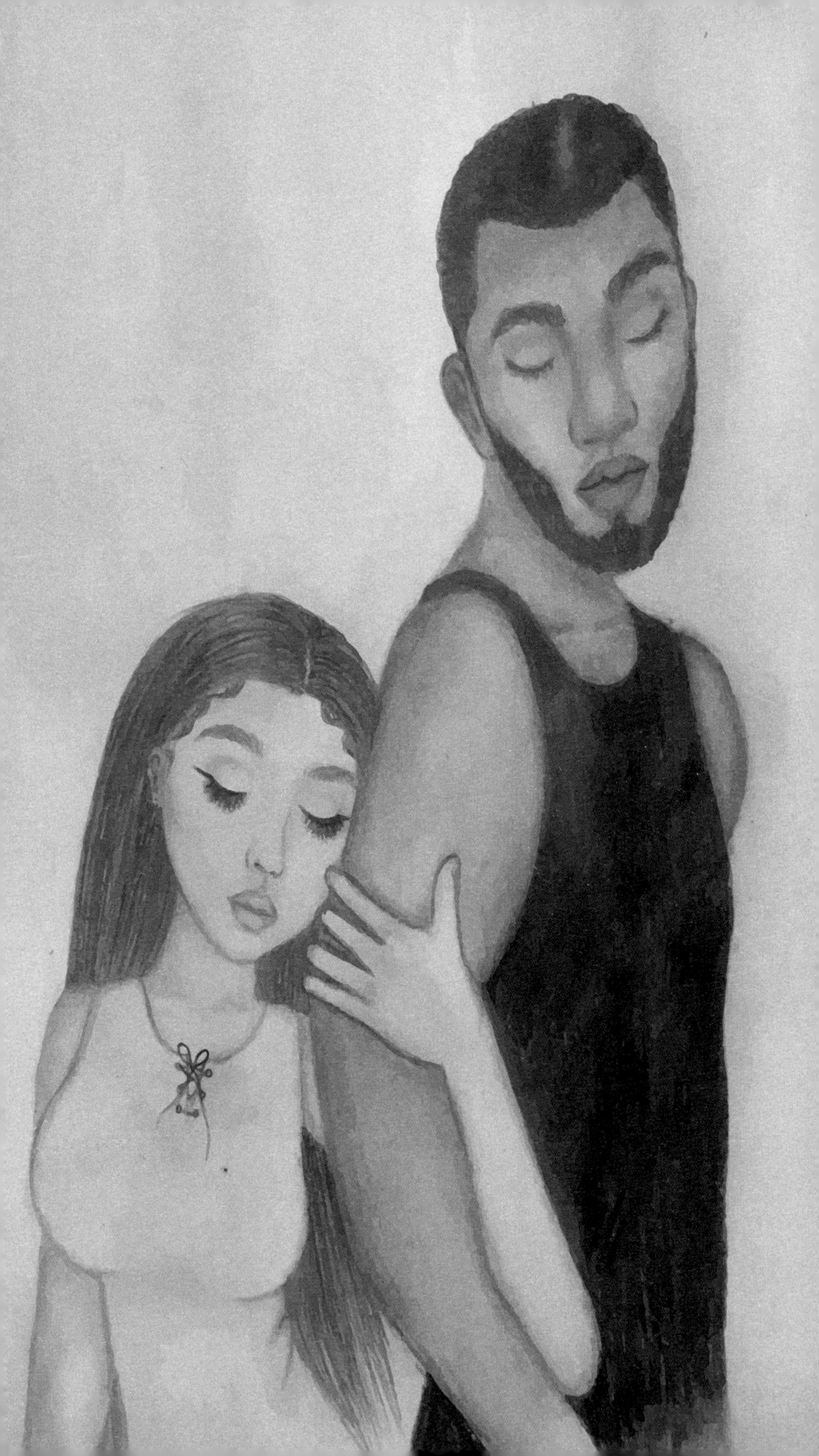

BY CANDLE LIGHT

The Lights are low,
and though we sit in a crowded room,
there is none but he and I.

The candle flickers,
my body shivers
as his fingers brush past my thigh.

The music plays,
and we're surrounded by the waves of sound
as we float on ecstasy

He is next to me,
And every single breath is a symphony
He is my perfect key.

He is my love,
and he was sent from above
to send tingles down my spine.

My insides explode,
Cuz, he knows my code
and he hits it every time.

One caress of my neck,
there's a cause and effect
while we linger eye to eye

Our spirits collide as I slip and slide
carried away by the tide,
I am high

Diving into you,
free falling through
the windows of your soul

You reach into the depth of me,
Your love has made whole.

THE ONE

The entity that completes me,
That envelopes the very soul,
the very heart, of this my existence.

My body created from the dust of the earth
Becomes the embankment through which streams of love flow
From the source of command
from the sea of you,

Whom are the son of Adam
For whose purpose I was formed,
Who reduced himself to increase me so
In time, I and he could once again become we.

Completion is now.

"Friends, the family we choose for ourselves"

FRIEND

I've not had the chance to thank you
Or the freedom to say I love you
But trust me, I truly do

Because of you my grey skies conceded to hints of blue
Because though unspoken I knew
that reflected in your eyes was my unlimited value

You saw me!
Even when surrounded by more obvious beauty
you chose the diamond hidden in the dirt,
the one that needed work to understand its worth

You took the time to know me!
Unaware that your tenderness and care
was the key to prepare me for my future,
of which you will always be a part
because the image of your love
is engraved on my heart.

For it's true and unconditional
And though we move on
and our childhood has gone,
the past can never be erased.

Because in those days,
engaging in friendship with you
I found my breakthrough

so though I've not had the chance to say thank you
or the freedom to say I love you

I want you to know that I truly do!

BABY GIRL

You cry baby girl,
and I understand why.
The love you deserved
you feel past you by

But I need you to know
you are not to blame
there's justification
at the route of your pain.

A bundle of purpose,
of beauty and grace,
born to a couple
of differing race

unable to cope
with the gift they beheld
they fumbled and stumbled
but still felt expelled

From the gift of adjustment,
the instinct of care
Personal demons
determined to bare

their intention to extinguish
destiny's call
but your heavenly father
would not let you fall.

Too important to end
in the form of a draft
there's a story unwritten
a discoverable craft.

So walk in your light
unaffected by the trial
A time will come
when they break free from denial

but the concern isn't yours
your commission is to grow
spread your wings baby girl
and soar as you go

SOMETIMES; LOVE HURTS

There is supposed to be an invisible bond that connects us, protects us from moving apart but in actual fact, what it does is allows you to rip and tear at my heart. To claw at it, like a lion on its pray its unsuspected because with each new day I love you, and I imagine you feel the same, that the pain I feel from thinking I'm not enough is merely a mistruth I've made up. But no, it's true, I am just above nothing to you. And though I continually hope for change, sometimes we must just accept that change may not come. And that in fact I may be the only one who sees my value.

ACTIVITY 3

Just for fun!

Let's imagine that you agree with the attributes of love as suggested by 1st Corinthians 13 4-7 (page 52). Use the table on the following page to measure how 'loving' you really are.

How many of these attributes do you bring to the relationships with the people you say you love? Maybe there are areas you need to work on to show true love.

a) Place the name of a loved one at the top of the column and simply tick the box of the attributes that you bring to that particular relationship (answers may differ between people).

b) Once you have completed your list you may want to consider the reasons behind your answers? Do you love people in different ways? Do you base your love for an individual on the things they do for you or is it unconditional? Does the love you feel from a person correlate with the love you give to them? Do you really even show love at all?

	LOVED ONE		
LOVE IS...			
Patient			
Kind			
Does not envy			
Does not boast			
Is not proud			
Does not dishonour			
Is not self-seeking			
Is not easily angered			
Keeps no record of wrongs			
Does not delight in evil			
Rejoices with the truth			
Always protects			
Always trusts			
Always hopes			
Always perseveres			

	LOVED ONE		
LOVE IS...			
Patient			
Kind			
Does not envy			
Does not boast			
Is not proud			
Does not dishonour			
Is not self-seeking			
Is not easily angered			
Keeps no record of wrongs			
Does not delight in evil			
Rejoices with the truth			
Always protects			
Always trusts			
Always hopes			
Always perseveres			

IDENTITY

'The purposes of a man's heart are deep waters, but one who has insight draws them out'

Proverbs 20:5

IDENTITY

Understanding identity is an extremely complex matter. To even begin to unravel it in the written form is like attempting to write this book in a foreign language, but here is what I understand.

Identity is often explained in terms of ethnicity, nationality, race, gender or religion. Many individuals link their identity to a job or career. We hear people talking about Identifying as; a black man, a builder, a musician, a woman or so on but these things are only a part of who a person is or what they do.

I believe that true identity is holistic and is inseparable from an individual's purpose.

There is a reason for your existence. There is something specific you were created to accomplish and achieve. Understanding this is the basis to understanding who you are.

A lack of personal identity breeds internal conflict, confusion and doubt whereas knowing ones identity brings a sense of belonging and wellbeing.

Identity is the you, you were created to be not necessarily the you, you have been shaped to be.

I AM

I am beautiful, and I don't care what you say
I am awesome in every single way

I was chosen to impact this earth
Before the moments of conception or birth

I am gifted, unique in my craft
The impeccable, original draft

I am exceptional, creative and wise
Strong, I overcome, I rise

I am everything, I can dream of and more
With the power to decide how high I soar

I am kind and compassionate too
Sincere in all that I do

I am honest and believe it or not,
Not pompous, I just know what I've got

And I declare it, proud and clear
So my ears will continually hear

And remind my heart to acknowledge the fact
That I am artistry and that is that

"The past does not define you, it merely stands as a catapult into your future."

WALKING BLIND

Suddenly I realise
that all this time I have been walking blind.
That I have been my own enemy,
embracing negativity,
grasping rejection as protection from myself.

Suddenly I begin to see,
that all the good I long for
is already embedded within me.
Beauty and creativity displayed freely
Dismissed as merely a universal ability.

Suddenly I understand
That God, by his own hand
Crafted from the sand a perfect being
Every inch encoded with profound meaning
Unique in its construction delicate in production
My function is flawless.

Suddenly I recognise that I should no longer disguise
The completeness of my soul
But declare to the world that I AM WHOLE

PURPOSE FILLED BEAUTY

Imagine with me
as this cycle of purpose filled beauty begins a fresh.
As you and me, we step in to our ordained destiny.

Women, we are the beginning of the journey
Continuation, without contemplation is dependent upon our vocation
As we house creation and birth a nation

Our sensational capacity and steely tenacity
Enables our solution of restitution within a heavenly constitution.

Pollution of our mind, designed to supress, we must confess, we stress as desirable qualities
Yet great qualities in us exist, if we'll only persist

Endurable strength, unconditional love, we are instinctively protective, courageous,
And above all else, selfless.

God showers us with powers that we can only ever gain when we call upon the name of Jesus.
Jesus our saviour allows us to savour in his beauty
Bathe in the rays of his glory.
The beholder sees more than we could ever be alone.

We are gifted, unrestricted. Creative with initiative.
Born perfectly with a purpose, reborn completely into purpose.

A WOMAN FOR EVERY SEASON

Woman
Beautiful Woman
Beautiful, Elegant, Distinguished Woman
Woman
Youthful Woman
Youthful, Brilliant, Resilient Woman
Woman
Virtuous Woman
Virtuous, Elected, Protected Woman
Sensitive Woman,
Fruitful Woman,
Extra – Ordinary Woman

A woman for every season
And for every season a particular reason.
A reason why you hold such exceptional traits
Each specific, personal, yet intentionally innate.

Innate in the sense it's ordained before birth
From the point at which Adam was formed from the earth.
Special was the blueprint, the completion of race
Yet multiplication, continuation, a revelation of Grace.

Ageless we mature, selfless we endure,
Priceless yet redeemed with a life
Jesus our Royal sacrifice.

A woman for every season
And for every season there is a reason
A reason why we look back and feel expelled
When actually we should feel compelled
To change our position,
Use the past as revision
Preventing repetition of a place we no-longer belong.

The ending of a phase is the beginning of a new Praise,
Be excited for the days are light and our future is bright
Let's delight in the roads set before

For embedded in one existence code is a most honourable mould
The mould through which Hannah, Mary and Esther came
Agendas so different but exactly the same

You see whatever plane of life you're on
And whatever season you look upon
Destiny has shone, proclaiming woman
Seasons are to go through and move from.

So in all things walk with your head held high,
Lest you shy away from greatness,
And the essence of limitless class.
Display your multiple facets in perfect cohesion
For you're an exceptional woman
Shining through your season

MORE THAN ENOUGH

Can she ever be enough?
Is she enough?

Continually she tries
Try's to push beyond the barries
To break through the bolted doors
To rise above the conditions
of generational, hereditary laws

To look past the black and white
And to love in full colour
She fights with her might
to be hailed a good mother

She speaks to the lost,
to the lonely and afraid
She comforts her children
despite mistakes they have made

She gifts them her all
to ensure they lack none
She smooths out their pain
till the heartache has gone

She lives compassion
and steps out on grace
She consoles the poor
with the greatest embrace

She is first to respond
when a conrad is down
She fumbles through the dirt
to recover their crown.

She is more than enough,
she just doesn't understand
Because loneliness
has now taken her hand

He leads her into paths that are grey
He speaks death to her soul every single day
Saying... you are unloved,
you will always be dismissed,
You ae imperfect,
your value will forever be missed

You are a failure, you are useless,
you're pathetic, you are a mess
You're a disappointment, unstable
But in your deepest distress

Recognise that this isn't true
That these feeling are not unique to you.
In fact this belief is the greatest of lies
So disregard all it implies

You are not alone in your feelings
You are not alone in your pain
You are not alone in your actions
You are not alone in your shame

The commonality of seasons
Is a guided tour of life
and though the journey may be bumpy
You will make it through alright

BEAUTIFUL YOU *BY TANYA MAYNARD*

Look at You, beautiful you
Over there and you wonder why we stare
Look at you, beautiful you
With your radiance and flare

Look at you, Powerful you with strength so dominant
you make us care
Look at you powerful you
You make the ignorant aware

Look at you, sassy you
Couldn't hide your pride or put yourself aside
Look at you, sassy you
Govern your heart, keep it kind

Look at you, angry you
Bubbling and boiling a plot of revenge you're foiling
Look at you, angry you
A greater cause will be your calling

Look at you , stubborn you
Rigid in your ways
Look at you, stubborn you
Committed you'll stay, you're loyalty will pay

Look at you, intelligent you
So articulate, you're not the fool
Look at you, intelligent you
You'll make your mark, don't loose your cool

Look at you, creative you
Bringing out of nothing, something new
Look at you, creative you
Taking bold new steps to tell us whats true

Look at you, look at you, Look at you

"I am as pepper in the midst of salt. On a mission to enforce my individuality when surrounded by normality"

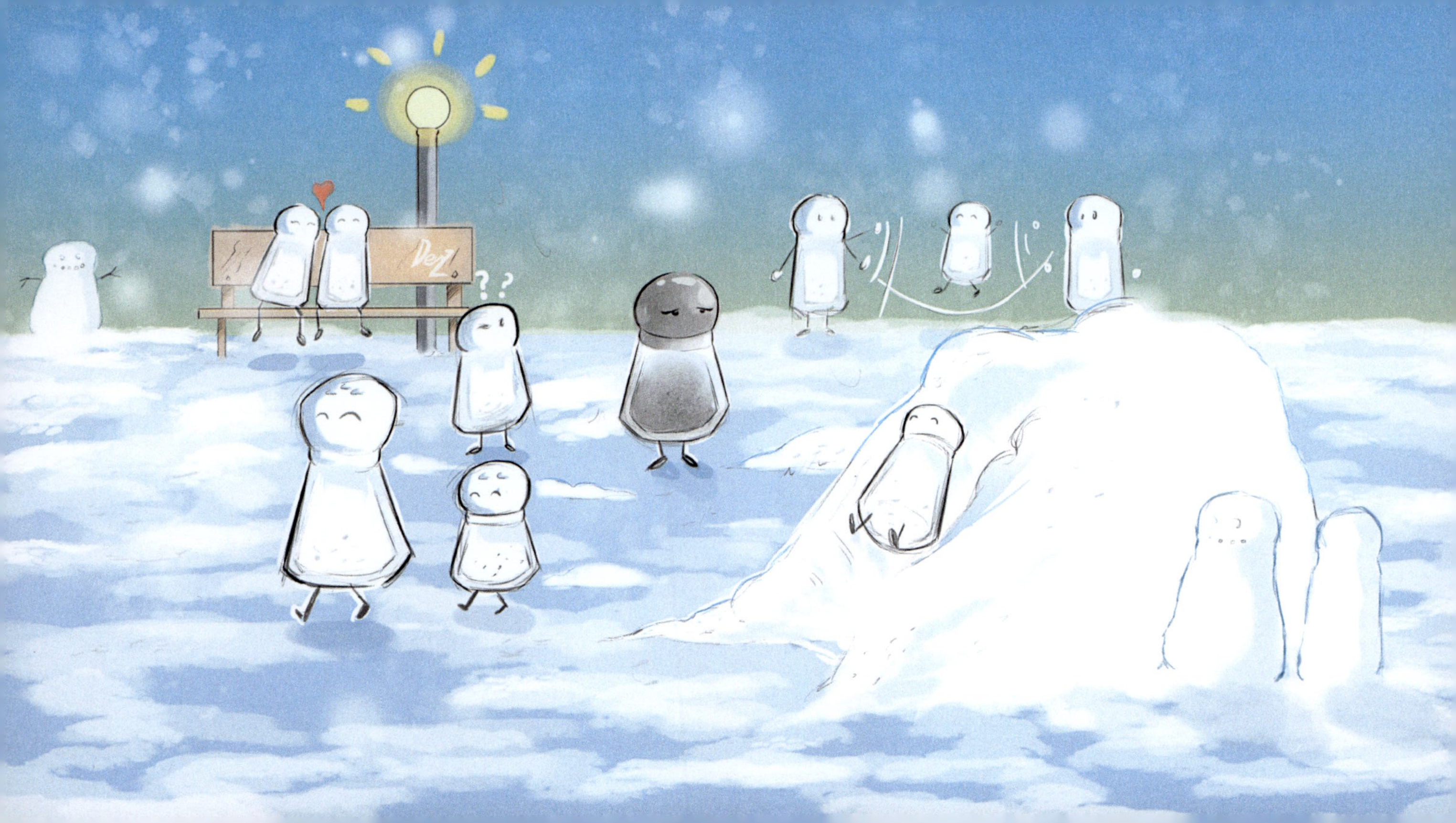

OVERCOME

Understand that those years of suppression and depression were more than that,
They were a rising up of our people.

If we fail to realise this,
then how can we resist
the temptation of retaliation
in a manner that has no power.

Knowledge and wisdom,
experience cohesion; unity.
Inherited weapons of our identity.

Know that we stand before and after an entourage of people resilient and strong.

The wrongs of our past,
present the edge in our future.
For now, we know how to win.

Together we stand, divided we fall
United, we overcome once more.

RAINBOW

I close my eyes
I see colours in the atmosphere
Open my eyes
I see hatred and reckless fear

I shut my eyes
I see peace and Love Supreme
Open my eyes
All I see is a darkened screen

Replaying images of past,
the future gone
Of when you held me down
and beat me till my life was none

And though I lived, you know
my spirit and my soul were dead
But for my execution,
no remorse, no tear was shed

But that's ok,
I don't repay
your wickedness with hate
We're products of society's induced mental state

I'm in the line of fire
My heart rate's getting higher
Now my desire
Is to find out why

I close my eyes
I fast forward to a time of peace
Open my eyes
Question did this hatred ever cease

I shut my eyes
I see unity all men are free
Open my eyes to lies,
corruption of our liberty.

Slavery, by definition a condition of
Implied supremacy,
cast systems propped by treachery

Expectancy for change,
rising up from our remains
A total fallacy,
Reality a bondage shaped key

When Martin spoke
He never dreamt that this would be the case
Total 360 of mankind and of the human race
The problem is
that even though you may unlock a chain
To simply wipe the surface

does not remove the stain.

So, as I look I wonder
what will help this system grow
To stop existing
in this never-ending Truman show

I'm in the line of fire,
My heart rates getting higher
now my heart's desire
is to find out why...

When Martin spoke
He never dreamt that this would be the case
Total 360 of mankind and of the human race
The problem is
that even though you may unlock a chain
To simply wipe the surface
does not remove the stain

Let's come together
and eradicate this senseless shame
Let's stand united,
let the rainbow guide us again.

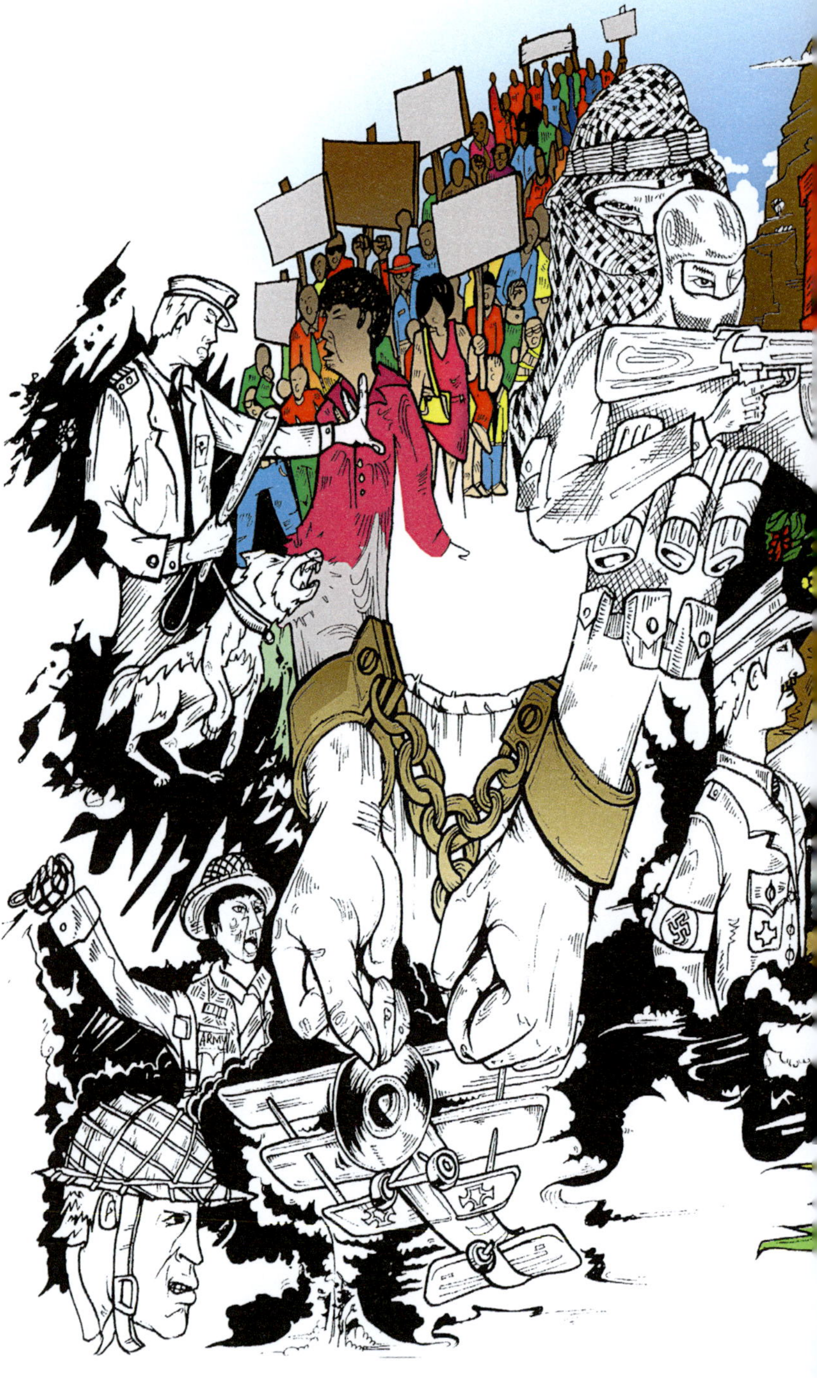
ARMY

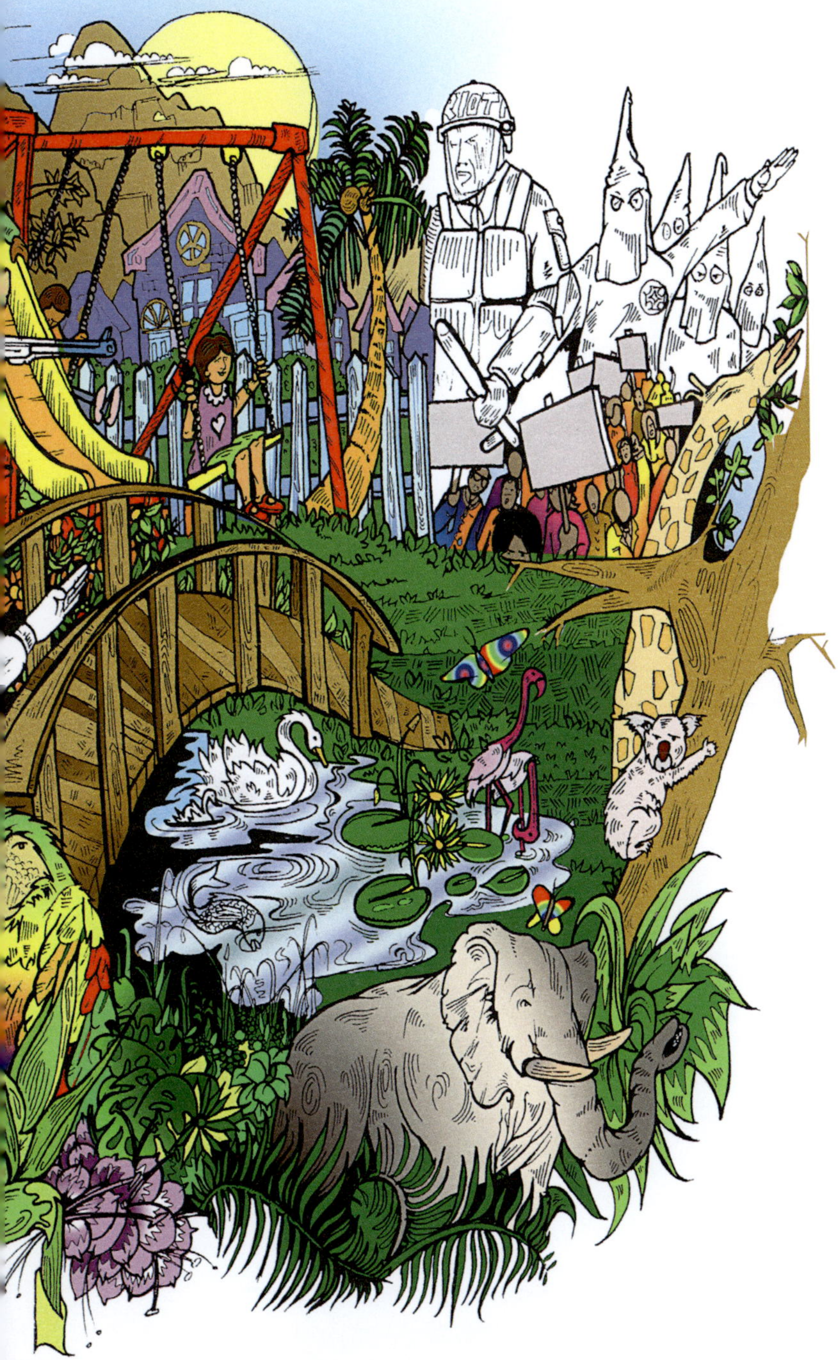
RIOT

I have a dream

"Free at last! Free at last! Thank God Almighty, we are free at last!"

PURPOSE PRINCIPLE

Do we live according
to what our values say
Are we moral or ethical
in every honest way

Do we look for what's important
And run with what we find
Or are we comfortable in leaving
All our principles behind

Do we enjoy to endure
For a conversation piece
Or are we genuinely searching
For a means to increase

Do we lean to our beliefs
And let success be our goal
Or do we hide amongst complaint
And basically prostitute our soul

Do we enjoy to be appressed
As a way to apportion blame
Or are we genuinely striving
To win our inner game

VALUES

To answer the question 'who am I?' seems pretty simple, however when it comes down to it, many people fumble over knowing what to say. I think this is because we don't often take the time to really evaluate our lives, we just get on with the action of living.

As I have mentioned before, in order to live your best life, it is important to know what you stand for, to identify your personal values and moral code. When you fail to honour these values you become dissatisfied and unfulfilled because you are no longer living your truth. You are no-longer living in your purpose but rather towards the expectations of others.

The next activity will help you identify the values that are important to you, then solidify the reasons why.

Understanding and accepting your values puts you on course to living the happy and fulfilled life you desire because it directs your purpose.

> "when we use our values to make decisions we make a deliberate choice to focus on what is important to us"

ACTIVITY 4

a) Read through the values table on the next page. Highlight or underline all the values that are important to you (use the blank spaces to add any values you think are missing).

From your chosen values:
b) Identify your top five and place them here, in order of importance. These are your core values.

1 _____

2 _____

3 _____

4 _____

5 _____

Acceptance	Fast pace	Power	Achievement	Financial rewards	Privacy
Ambition	Friendship	Reaching potential	Appreciation	Fun	Recognition
Harmony	Responsibility	Autonomy	Heath	Results	Balance
Romance	Belonging	Humour	Routine	Challenge	Imagination
Collaboration	Influence	Service	Commitment	Intellect	Sharing
Justice	Spirituality	Competition	Kindness	Status	Connection
Teaching	Creativity	Love	Team work	Equality	Loyalty
Excitement	Travel	Expertise	Nurturing	Trust	Fairness
Winning	Fame	Peace	Wisdom	Family	Personal growth
Adventure	Focus	Community	Intuition	Productivity	Prospects
Authenticity	Happiness	Leadership	Success	Respect	Authority
Helping others	Risk taking	Tolerance	Excellence	Beauty	Honesty
Security	Choice	Order	Variety	Independence	Self-expression
Zest for life	Compassion	Solitude	Learning	Contribution	Tradition
Making a difference	Passion	Faith			

c) Write a short paragraph for each value stating why it is important to you (what does it mean to you?).

1 _____
_____
_____
_____

2 _____
_____
_____
_____

3 _____
_____
_____
_____

4

_____

_____

_____

_____

5

_____

_____

_____

_____

d) Now rate each of these values using a scale of 1 – 10 to indicate the extent to which each value is currently present in your life (10 meaning fully present and 1 meaning not present at all).

Value	Score

If you are honest about your answers, the higher the scores the happier you are.

Thinking about the reasons for your scores, consider which areas in your life are not matching up to your core values. For example; this could be in relation to your job/career, family life, partner or spouse, friendship groups or religious beliefs.

What things do you need to change to align your actions to your values and in doing so, begin to live a more purpose driven, focussed and fulfilled life.

SOLDIER

The battle is over, earthly soldier
Spiritual warrior
You are now more than a conqueror.
For you go to reside
Beside the King of Kings and the Lord of Lords
For yours is the kingdom of heaven
Because, righteousness is what was required
And a faithfulness which never grew tired
And a boldness to continue to fight
And fervently stand for what is right
keeping this in sight
your life became a light,
a beacon through the night
now in completion of this task
you pass on a legacy
saturated in beauty

and as you fly, accelerating high
above the perforated clouds in the sky
waving goodbye to this temporary state
obliterating the bate of this fleshy weight
take your stand in a band of heavenly hosts
boast in a force, strengthened by a source of unquenchable power
shower in drops of glory
for your story has just begun
and in His-story the battle is won
so now rest, in the radiance of the son
for in death you have overcome
the battle is won.

WALK IN POWER

Slowly inching away
Peeling back the decay
of the layer which sits upon our truth.

It is beautiful,
like the most precious of stones,
Strong.
It externally glows flawless.

Polished in perfection
yet protecting deception
Its value is hidden.

Hidden beneath the make-up
and the kiss of the sun
Behind the silver and gold,
Beside the stories cunningly told
to uphold the notion of stature, status and class
Hiding the system of cast.

Outward displays are the rage,
or should I say the craze
of a society so fixated on the external
Focused on the idea of eternal youth

To never grow old
is an ode to humanities glory,
A complete none address
of the mess overtaking morality.

Paralysis in motion.

COMPASSION'S GAME

Pull away the layers of reason
Demolish the tower of excuses
Tamper with the bed of dismissal
And throw away the flag of acquittal

Blissfulness can no-longer be a foundation of ignorance
A little donation no-longer the appeasement of guilt
or the sacrificial offering to shame
This game has been played for far too long.

Acceptance of murder and racism
of prejudice and pride
of power and money
have crucified life.
Sent a tidal wave of destruction
with permission to flow like cement
Crashing down on hope,
swallowing love,
imprisoning its strength.

We need to lament for this earth!

For compassion has gone,
overtaken by survival
Fear has climbed the ranks of emotion and feelings and
taken its position in the seat of authority
by overthrowing humanity.
This is blasphemy of the highest degree.

Take back your power!

The destructive grip of darkness seeks to devour the simplicity of being and the exquisiteness of light

Capture the sun and run away from solitude
ingest its magnitude,

Open the mouth and let flow justice and peace, goodness and unity
Declare equality, share prosperity, champion serenity

Quiet the dampening of acquired senselessness
march relentlessly towards change,
embrace the future and erase obliterative prophesy.

Oversee emancipation and deliver us into the hands of creations intention.

Discovering once again unsolicited compassion.

CRISIS

My heart cries for a wold that's in pain
Numbness has dampened shame
From the belly of darkness
the fragrance of hate rises
like steam in a boiling pot of rage
its fury is uncomfortable, unquenchable
forgiveness subsequential but essential
for progress, for change.

Drain the blockage of the mind,
find the disease, administer the cure
scold the wicked, relinquish the war
still the ripple, deactivate the flow of the fickle
for its tide breaks beside the body of the dead sea
symbolically the effervescence of cruelty settles beside
the shore, upon the rocks and the cliffs
beneath the foliage pitilessly dismissed by the suffocating stench of the forgotten.

Demonstrate compassion, invoke empathy,
solicit understanding.
Attempt to gain access to the place within,
hidden below the hairs of the skin.
Force them to stand to attention,
in re-sensitisation to what is clearly wrong,
of what is sincerely brutal
and devastatingly strong willed.

The power to change is entrusted to the many

yet perverted by the very few who believe they are entitled,

believe they are a heightened level of species

pretentiously portraying that their faeces run gold

It is a lie! Wickedness swallowed
creating excrement so consuming
that it bypasses the place of morality
and is vomited out in dollar coated political calamity.

Words that mean nothing but yet provoke so much.
Jealousy and greed, starvation and selfish need
played out upon the humble,
the innocent and simple in heart.

The part of the understudy has already been cast,
permitted to dictate the manifestation of hate
via our inability and unwillingness to move.

BUT, the lead role is free
and waiting to be moulded and shaped into equality,
thanksgiving and love.

MAKE A START

I am so confused
I don't know where to start
How to mend the cracks
Repair the broken hearts

Travelling in circles
Chasing priority's shifts
Lagging behind action
Paralysed and stiff

Prepared to engage warfare
if stood on guaranteed success
For war produces martyrs
And I'm afraid to lay in rest

What change can be made
From the bottom of the ground
Consumed by earth where
Silence is sound

To raise my voice
Is to cleanse the air
To speak up for justice
And seize what is fair

For those who suffer
Are in need of reprieve
I'm downloaded with answers

But now I must breathe

Stock taking the knowledge
Letting wisdom be guide
To share what is hidden
Expose the inside

I am so irritated,
I don't know where to start
The promise land beckons
But the path is not marked

Yet, the internal map
Signals where I should go
Step out in faith
And my instincts will flow

Simplicity is underrated
When destiny calls
Clarity is not the defining clause

When counting the magnitude
Of what's to be done
Overwhelming feelings may overcome
Doubts and fears teeter at the brim
Excuses now tactics for stalling

It's true I may not know where to start
But I will release the pressure
And just follow your heart

GOD

GOD

When I look out my bedroom window and open my eyes to blue sky, green grass and nesting birds I am often overwhelmed. It is beautiful! Everything has order, has life and the capacity to reproduce.
The creativity of human kind and our ability to invent the impossible; the incredible, indescribable entity of the spirit and soul and its intangible yet powerful essence all points toward the existence of a higher power.

This higher power is who I call God. The creator of earth and space, the beginning and ending of all things. The author of time and the instructor of order. An entity more powerful than we can fully comprehend. A source of Hope.

As you may have gleaned whilst reading this book, I had a strong, Christian, church upbringing and many of the poems in this section are reflective of this. They highlight possible struggles between religious opinion and internal truth and about our value and identity as intended by the creator.

Whatever our thoughts of God, what is, is and what isn't, just isn't. Therefore, don't simply accept what you are told. Do not allow fear to prevent you from seeking truth, because to find truth is to find knowledge and knowledge is power. The power to live in happiness, the power to live fulfilled the power to make change.

"Ask and it will be given to you; seek and you will find; knock and the door will be opened to you. For everyone who asks receives; the one who seeks finds; and to the one who knocks, the door will be opened."

Matthew 7:7-8

BLESSED IS THE ONE WHO FINDS WISDOM

'Blessed is the one who finds wisdom, and the one who gets understanding, for the gain from her is better than gain from silver and her profit better than gold.

She is more precious than jewels, and nothing you desire can compare with her.

Long life is in her right hand; in her left hand are riches and honour.

Her ways are ways of pleasantness, and all her paths are peace.

She is a tree of life to those who lay hold of her; those who hold her fast are called blessed.'

Proverbs 3:13-18 ESV

DISCOVERING EARTH
BY HANNAH-MARIE MCLEAN PYLE
Age 10

Fun with friends
Play and pals
Those things make me smile
Cute little kittens
Fabulous festivities
Keep me laughing all the while

In God's world of happy things
Many things can bring me joy.
Grand trees blossom and flowers bloom
Across the world as we all look up at the shining moon

A shiny moon which does not shine,
till night has come, day left behind
I lose myself in its beauty
As birds sing and natures bells ring
Finding myself again, and even then, the wind whistles sweetly
Blow, blow, blow, blow.

THROUGH GODS EYES
(You Are)

Beautiful!
Do you know who you are?
You are awesome!
Like the twinkle in a star
you are perfect!
A reflection of my heart.
I started a revolution in you

You are special!
From the beginning of all days,
you were destined
to be the catalyst for my praise
and in every phase
of creation I knew
that my greatest work would be you!

Because you are fearfully
and wonderfully made.
You are valuable
worth more than the price I paid
Hand crafted
with the greatest of love
My spirit I sent descending from above
to draw you closer to me
So you can see that you are

Beautiful!
Please know who you are?
You are awesome!
like the twinkle in a star
You are perfect!
A reflection of my heart.
My revolution starts in you

AFRAID

I'm afraid that my world will crumble
If I really humble myself to my beliefs
I say that I know God and that I do
But Jesus do I really know you?

I call your name, I invest in this game
Of faith and accepting your truths
But when I ask for your guidance
And my face hits the ground
It seems, you are nowhere to be found

I pray for your input, I ask for your help
But not much seems to go to plan
and the Christian response to my now broken trust
Is simply 'God's ways are not that of man'

Though I hear your response and explore your reply
There's something that just won't compute
Why pray and have hope if my request holds no weight?
This is something that I must refute

So, I study my word and I consider my hope
And the two don't appear to agree
For the thing that I struggle to truly accept
Is that Christ is exactly like me

Understanding the power of humankind
Means: I am more than a robot adrift

A man wrapped in flesh with a conscious and choice
Free will both a curse and a gift

The discernment within, when I focus on Him
Is the thing that directs my way
And the answers I seek when I kneel down to pray
Are made real through the things that I say

So, if I'm honest the lack of evidence I see
Is no less than an excuse
since everything I could want or need
I have the authority to bind up or loose

It seems like its fear with a touch of control
That restricts me form reaching my goal
As the words that I speak that give life and death
Are the same ones destroying my soul

So choice is the key to this minefield of life
Explosive encounters almost guaranteed
But the method for clearing that dangerous path
Is the knowledge:
We have everything we need to succeed!

I'm afraid my world will crumble
If I humble myself to my beliefs
But the only way I will truly know
is to stop wondering and let actions release

GOD's Blueprint...
When you're on the right path everything you need will find you

DEEPER

I want you to go deeper,
I want you to go deeper into me
I want you to truly see that I am He
who created the heavens and the earth.
The moon and the sky
the stars that draw nigh
unto the call and cry of my heart.

Yet (they are) merely a tiny, miniscule part of my creation
of the expanse of my word,
see the formation as Nothing took note and heard.
Consider the moment of obedience
where dark turned to light
and took its position to govern the night

I want you to go deeper,
I want you to go deeper into me.
I want you to share in the vibrations
of the earth and the sea.

I want you to know who I am
both as God and as man
transcending the limits of a physical plan,
Sealed by the blood of a sacrificial lamb.

You were designed in my image,
perfection made whole
mind, body, spirit and soul.

I pumped blood through your veins
And breathed life to your heart
I determined the end as I did with the start.
My rainbow I left as a devotional mark
Of my promise to you.

Still, I need you to go deeper,
I need you to go deeper into me
I need you to recognise that
the purity of my word is the key

to survival and wonder, to miracles unseen
to tearing down religions acrimonious streams
of fear and confusion
confliction and doubt
of turning the winds on this spiritual drought
of breaking down barriers to crumbling walls
I am the way to penetrate unmovable doors.

I want you to go deeper,
I want you to go deeper into me
I want you to live forever unravelling the mystery
Discovering the simplicity of the blueprint of life
Existing completely in the best of me
As you assuredly move deeper into me.

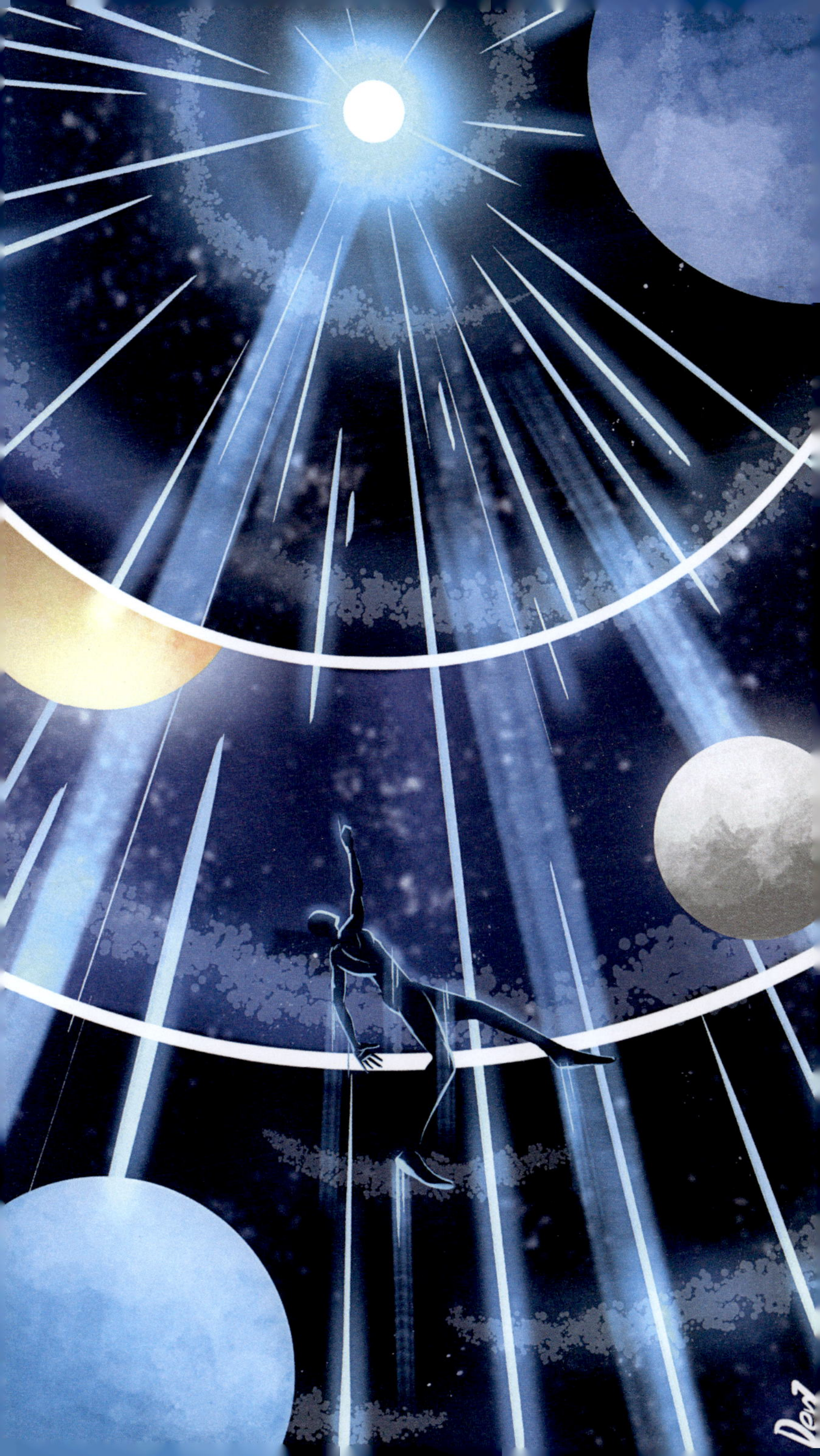

WRAPPED UP

Wrapped up in sin without realising
Compromising your Christianity,
Letting go of your sanity
For a fake reality of worldly vitality
Hyped up by ungodly vanity.

Prosperity and perceived beauty
Become key in your inability to be free
As your enemy plays on your naivety
Through the media and music TV
Engraving a false sense of security
Into your spiritual armoury
Breaking through the shadow of what is left of you
But who do you turn to
For you can't admit defeat
Complete the humiliation of the affiliation you've formed
Sitting on the wrong board
Changing weapons from a sword to a gun
But when all is said and done
The original weapon was the one
and is the one and is the one to come!

So, to save your face, God gave you grace
So, base the rest on this.
Dismiss your need for greed,
It only feeds the wrong man,
Creating the strongman to pull you down.
Instead, take your crown
And live profoundly in the grace
Of God.

CHRISTIAN REBUKE

I'm here to speak with you
because I'm sick of being embarrassed about who I am
Forgetting that I'm a child of the risen lamb
From the beginning I was in his plan
And for me he took the form of a man
To be stripped and whipped
Battered and bruised
and I must surely be confused
If I abuse his sacrifice.
So please take my advice
As His life paid the price

More importantly, I need to ask you a favour
To give due respect to our Lord and saviour
Don't just sit there, staring into thin air
Waiting for the Pastor to come and share
A word you never heard when He Spoke
God spoke,
But because it was through me
You failed to see
You crave for the ministers on TV
When Gods speaks for free.
He's here for free.

He equipped you and I
With the tools to live and not die
So please, please
Try to attain,
Strive to gain, to maintain holiness,
Brokenness.
Confess your sin.
The sin you allowed to move in
To reside within your temple.
The temple which you defile
Because in your denial
You actually believe that you can achieve
Any level of praise
Simply because you raise your hand
But yet you stand there
Pompous and proud,
Crying aloud, making the right sound
Hell bound!

We sing the words
I'm coming back to the heart of worship,
When it's all about you,
It's all about you…
I beg to question it's all about who?
because it seems wright now, it's all about you.
"fill me Lord, fill me Lord, fill me Lord too
What for?

Should he fill you so you can disrespect him some more
With your vain repetitions and religious traditions
Listen,
You don't have to beg,
receive your gift God said.

Before the words, He sees the heart
So, depart from your wicked ways
Enter into prosperous days.
Be assured that
When you place Him above all else
And selfish ways are gone
Zion will become your new name
And his dwelling place you will then proclaim
Is in fact, one and the same.

TESTIMONY REVISED

I was messed up, confused,
misused and abused,
and I refused to believe I was worthy of simply being me.

I felt oppressed and ashamed
so I blamed the world for my life
Me, a mother, a wife
still craving to be a child, acting wild, for attention and misplaced affection.

I became suppressed and distressed,
confined, unassigned,
diseased but blind to the cure.
Surely there is more to life than this?

I yearned inside, burned because of pride,
behind which destruction resigned,
until my eyes were opened to the truth.
At that point I realised, that

You and I, in Christ we fly
and if not, we die
but we still try for the high for its innate,
so, we recreate the act of worship to no avail
as we fail to understand,

Jesus is the key to perfect harmony and serenity within ourselves!

Knowing him is to know yourself,
Loving him is to love yourself.
This is my testimony
for now I see myself Completely free!

ACTIVITY SHEETS

Bad Seed	Negative Consequence	Action

	LOVED ONE		
LOVE IS...			
Patient			
Kind			
Does not envy			
Does not boast			
Is not proud			
Does not dishonour			
Is not self-seeking			
Is not easily angered			
Keeps no record of wrongs			
Does not delight in evil			
Rejoices with the truth			
Always protects			
Always trusts			
Always hopes			
Always perseveres			

Acceptance	Fast pace	Power	Achievement	Financial rewards	Privacy
Ambition	Friendship	Reaching potential	Appreciation	Fun	Recognition
Harmony	Responsibility	Autonomy	Heath	Results	Balance
Romance	Belonging	Humour	Routine	Challenge	Imagination
Collaboration	Influence	Service	Commitment	Intellect	Sharing
Justice	Spirituality	Competition	Kindness	Status	Connection
Teaching	Creativity	Love	Team work	Equality	Loyalty
Excitement	Travel	Expertise	Nurturing	Trust	Fairness
Winning	Fame	Peace	Wisdom	Family	Personal growth
Adventure	Focus	Community	Intuition	Productivity	Prospects
Authenticity	Happiness	Leadership	Success	Respect	Authority
Helping others	Risk taking	Tolerance	Excellence	Beauty	Honesty
Security	Choice	Order	Variety	Independence	Self-expression
Zest for life	Compassion	Solitude	Learning	Contribution	Tradition
Making a difference	Passion	Faith			

COMING SOON...

Gina's second book is well on the way!

In a story about adventure, mystery and discovery the main character Nevaeh is forced to face her fears head on whilst her world literally crumbles beneath her feet. Not knowing who she can trust, Nevaeh must travel this journey alone but the more she encounters the more she understands that nothing is as it seems.

A SNIPPET...

"I demand my life back", Nevaeh shouted as she banged on the solid oak door.

Overwhelming it stood tall and strong, with a seeming sense of honour it proudly fulfilled its duty guarding the mystical portal to the spirit realm. Encased in rout iron yet edged in the purest gold its brilliance was captivating, somewhat enticing. Nevaeh instantly understood that to pass through, to take that leap into the unknown would change her world forever.
Whether for good or bad her spirit bubbled in anticipa-

tion, every emotion, every bone in her body compelled her to break through.

"I demand back my life" Nevaeh shouted again but this time with a degree of caution... "Open up, I command you to open up!"
With that the door slowly began to shake. The force startled Nevaeh who jumped back and stumbled to the floor. Quickly scrambling to her feet she ran to the corner of the room, compressing her body into the crease of the wall. Though she knew there was nowhere she could hide its sturdiness and strength seem like her only possible place of refuge. With every movement of the widening door, the earth trembled more fiercely. The deafening sound relentless and unforgiving ripped through her ears finding a place within her mind susceptible to its torcher. As the door in all its authority and splendour, unapologetically took pride in its assignment, it was all Nevaeh could do to fight its control.
Then, without the slightest of warning everything stopped.
Complete Stillness!
An eerie silence filled the room and for the first time Nevaeh was afraid.

To explore future release dates or for information of all that is on offer from the author please visit ginamyrie.com

---

About the Author

Gina Myrie is a performing poet, life coach, and entrepreneur who has spent many years motivating and inspiring people from all backgrounds.

Gina believes that every individual is born with and for a purpose. They are destined to impact the world in a positive way, but many are often crippled by fear.

Gina aims to support and inspire individuals to step out of fear and into freedom, fulfilment and destiny.

(for further information go to ginamyrie.com)